Words Like
Fate and Pain

Words Like
Fate and Pain

Karen Fiser

𝖅

ZOLAND BOOKS

Cambridge, Massachusetts

First edition published in 1992 by
Zoland Books, Inc.
384 Huron Avenue
Cambridge, Massachusetts 02138

Library of Congress Cataloging-in-Publication Data

Fiser, Karen, 1945–   .
    Words like fate and pain / Karen Fiser. —1st ed.
        p.   cm.
    ISBN: 0-944072-23-2 : $9.95
    I. Title.
PS3556.I766W67   1992
811'.54—dc20   92-53832
                                      CIP

Second printing, March 1993
Printed in the USA by Braun-Brumfield, Inc., Ann Arbor, MI
Composed by Books International, Deatsville, AL
Book Design by Boskydell Studio

To the memory of my grandmother,
Myrtis Belle Allen Cunningham
Stars in her crown

Love is put to the test,
pain not.

— WITTGENSTEIN

ACKNOWLEDGMENTS

I am indebted to the editors of *The American Voice, Bakunin, The Green Mountains Review, Hanging Loose, Kaleidoscope, Walrus,* and *Zone 3,* where earlier versions of some of these poems first appeared.

I wish to thank the Creative Writing Department at Stanford University for awarding me the Wallace E. Stegner Fellowship which enabled me to complete this manuscript. I am most grateful to my fellow poets both at Stanford and at Mills College, for their friendship, support, and criticism. I am particularly indebted to Ann Neelon and Annie Stenzel. I owe special thanks to Benjamin Alire Sáenz, for his many acts of friendship; to Robin Wells, for her steadfast belief in me, and to Joellen Hiltbrand, whose courage and forthrightness were an example when I needed one. Thank you also to teachers who have shared their understanding of their art: Chana Bloch, Diana O'Hehir, Stephen Ratcliffe, Sandra McPherson, Kenneth Fields, and W.S. DiPiero. I wish especially to thank Denise Levertov for her kind and careful attention to my manuscript.

I want to express my love and respect for the community of persons with disabilities, for their strength, their anger, and their outrageous humor. They have taught me and kept me going. Special thanks to two amazing women, Gail Enman of the Cambridge Commission on Handicapped Persons and Marian Blackwell-Stratton of the Disability Rights Education Defense Fund.

Over the last few years in which these poems have been written, I have become more deeply aware how my life has been sustained by rare and wonderful friends. I am so pleased to have this chance to acknowledge three of them, without whose help I would not have survived to write: Anne Hall, Larry Blum, and my very gifted therapist, Lia Lund.

CONTENTS

Part One

Across the Border

For you there was no conscious departure,
no hurried packing for exile.
You are here, anyway, in your own
minor archipelago of pain.

Do what every exile does. Tell stories.
Smuggle messages across the border.
Remember things back there
as simpler than they ever were.

The Short Song of What Befalls

—*for* ROBIN WELLS

What just happens, the mystery of that,
what comes about apart from trying.
Accidere: to happen, generally
of misfortunes. Perhaps better, to befall.
By the Interstate I saw one red
high heeled shoe and wondered did she lose it
running from the car very late at night,
did she try to escape what was happening to her?
Was she walking on the shoulder,
did the car run her down,
and the shoe was left behind in the accident?
Did she throw it at the driver's head
in a rage and miss and lose the shoe
out the window, like that? So her misfortune
was just losing the shoe. On a radio interview
I heard a woman, one of five
struck by lightning in Ohio,
whose eyes changed instantly from blue
to grey. This befell her
in the late afternoon. Now she lives on
in terror of the rain,
she knows what any storm can do.

Wheelchairs That Kneel Down
Like Elephants

Last night I rode a tightrope
with my wheelchair. No net.
The night before, I left my body
on the steep ground with its pain.
I walked again by leaning,
elbows careless on the wind,
hitching myself along in light surprise.
Days I am heavy,
a clumsy bear on wheels,
bumping into things
and smiling, smiling. Nights
I invent new means of locomotion:
flying velocipedes, sailcars,
wheelchairs that kneel down
like elephants, carry me carefully
up the long stairs. Intricate
engines of need and night and air.

Night Shift

At first
it is the same nightmare:
the pain factory
deep in the interior,
the blast furnace going
half the night,
driving the muffled
engines to make enough
hurt.   Two dark
towers engage
the milky sky. Uncanny
light pours out from the heart
of the furnace.

The dream turns.
Suddenly, tiny in the great factory,
sliding through terrifying
gears and wheels unharmed,
defiant: Chaplin.

No, this is false
transcendence. You notice
Chaplin isn't changed
by any suffering, never
has to learn to live
as changed. But you.

Like the night animal tearing
in the teeth of the pain
machinery, you will not
get out of this the same.

Words Like Fate and Pain

Ostalgia: this strange and perfect word
means bone pain, but it carries my regret,
it is freighted like the word *Saudades*
Elizabeth Bishop loved, meaning homesickness,
longing for a place, missing your friends.
The word evokes the hospital, lighted up like an ocean liner
bearing me on and on through the dark,
its windows cool to the feverish touch, it calls back
whispered consultations, and a faint throbbing
of engines somewhere deep within the building.
The sound of it brings sorrow for the one I was
and had to leave in that place
as if I were driving away from my friend for the last time,
leaving her standing there, finite and brave,
her body diminishing in the mirror.
It brings the steady ticking of the winter rains,
the water glass beside the bed, your small cool hands
before you left, and the silence.
It conjures for me even the wild panicked smell
of pain too great to bear, when the fragile soul
goes under suddenly, without a word.

Slow Freight

Swelling bone my boxcars
jolt down the steep track
of night. They click and sway
around the long deep curve
of the thirsty hours, then far
across pale rumpled sheets
of desert and slowly up into the aching
mountains, silvered face of rock
slanting away to the empty lairs
of animals who spend their nights
outside awake. The dry stars observe
from their freezing distances.

Stranded

Gasping at the bed's edge
you cling to the sour pillow
of sand, flounder through
the briny sheets, held
out of your damaged body's
element. You keep struggling
in the shallows for the right
kind of breath. Something
you can never fathom
drove you here. Think hard,
so hard it hurts.
Call out all you want.
You can't get back to the rest
of your life, to finish it.

The Prisoner

What if pain is the prisoner
of the body? What if it waits,
desperate, watches
for the opening to daylight.
Suppose that familiar ache
lies sleepless on its back
all night, thinking
of the life it led before.

The pain has to remember to eat.
It is writing a memoir, pacing.
It refuses to give up.

Pointing to the Place of the Pain

Do we know the place of pain in Euclidean space,
so that when we know where we have pains we know
how far away from two of the walls of this room,
and from the floor."
        —WITTGENSTEIN, *The Blue Book*

You keep thinking of pain as a place
you could leave, walk out
and slam the last heavy door on.
Then you would be whole, returned
magically to life like Tony Curtis
playing Houdini, locked in the trunk
at the lake bottom, many takes
to make his escape look perfect.
You could breathe again.

Imagine the pain you inhabit as a region
in between, ineluctably your own
like your softest skin or the space of freedom
where your memories happen, a room
no one else can come into,
however close they try to stand.

How strange that only feeling
could keep you in this place,
quiet and wounded and intent as the air is
around real suffering,
the pool of silence spreading out
from the hospital bed.

What Happened to You?

The moment he sees me, he comes running into the peaceful
    suburban street,
hands up, palms out, a little sternly as if he's stopping
    traffic.
He trots along beside my chair. "What happened to you?"
    he asks,
serious six-year-old eyes fixed on my legs. He really wants
    to know.

Most children want to ask. Even the little ones, rolling by
    in their strollers,
look at me with round eyes, as if they wonder how I get to
    have wheels, too.
I look back at them, trying to see what looks so different.
    How they know.
Sometimes they ask if it hurts. Once a small boy asked me,
    "Are you going to die?"

I hardly ever mind, or I try not to mind. It's important
    to be matter-of-fact
and calm. I want them to know this is part of the story.
    But this afternoon,
with the quiet leaves sifting all around, when he asks his
    important question
I want to cry and scream and break down in the street:
    I don't know, I don't know.

That Other Life

I want to live in all those other houses.
Boarded-up cottages on the beach at the Cape,
student dumps with apple crate shelves.
The narrow, blistered shotgun house
somebody lived a hard life in and had to
abandon suddenly, closet doors gaping.
That fine adobe north of Albuquerque
painted true magenta. Houses with steep stairs,
though I can't climb. A silver Airstream
not far from the Pedernales. Long, dusty
railroad flats, Cambridge tripledeckers,
back halls smelling like old wax,
cabbage, Irish grandmothers. I want
to strip the faded lilac paper,
scrub those sticky floors.
Fix them all up and move in. What then?
That other life always rises. Imaginary
houses beckon. In the dark brick heart
of Boston winter, I'd wake up dreaming
a house in Mississippi,
a white house with a tin roof, roses.

Not Down Here

I don't want to stay
down here, not
in this slow
chair. This amazing
consecration of a day
I should be swooping
over Oakland.
Going loop the loop.
Look at them glide
from the highest branch.
I want to go.
I want to practice landing
stacked right up
against a bird.

Rest Near Evening

An owl is laughing
through the gravity of sleep.
The quince flares in the heavy
yellow after rain.
Among the thick black bodies
of the trees, its flowers glow
jewel red with remnant light,
as if they refuse
to let it go. At last even
the light they hold leaks out
through the aperture of evening,
as it tightens down to dark.

Protect Yourself From This

Protect yourself from this, the sight
of the lumpish woman in plate glass
laboring to push herself along
in her coat, in the sun.
She looks to be a woman of a certain age,
a nice woman, but forlorn, with too much pain
in her face to be outdoors. You look away,
then swiftly back, to see her struggle with the chair
outside the heavy bank door, holding her packages upright
in her lap with her teeth.
She starts to mutter, how difficult
things are. For an instant you allow yourself to feel
her dread, her effort not to become
another crazy crying on a Berkeley street.

She is not what you feel yourself to be,
but what you see you are,
reflected in the world's unyielding surfaces.
You know you can never leave her, now.

What Comes Next

I am flying along the ground
in my wheelchair in the dark,
pushing fast around a huge lake.
It is taking me far too long.
I run into thick mud and roots,
my clotted wheels drag and slide
sideways in my grip. I have to leave
the chair and swing myself along
on my hands. I swing my body easily
as if I didn't have legs
any more, they're gone.
Eyes wide open in the dark
I rush past the last scattered lights
of houses like sparks streaming by.
What comes next is jerky and oddly lit
like the part where the townspeople
gather with their torches,
and the creature runs away,
cursing softly to itself.

The Way to be Immortal

The crow with the withered foot flies fine.
Insouciant among the greasy paper plates
and sandwich rinds, he works the patio lunch crowd
like a waiter playing at being a waiter.
Intent on bread, he does not concern himself
with what comes next. Why then do you
recall the old woman lying broken in the street,
her black shoe in a widening pool of blood,
the vivid daily fruit split open at the intersection?

In this mild weather you begin to have your death;
still it is good to sit in the shade and write
this second, unlooked-for life. Even in his old age,
his assistant said, Michelangelo would sit shoeless,
drawing for hours. Each working moment is complete,
perfectly equal to itself and right, if death came now.
Suddenly you know what those words meant
you copied long ago: *The way to be immortal is to die daily.*

Part Two

Ontological Relativity

"In practice of course we end the regress of coordinate
systems by something like pointing."
—W.V.O. QUINE

That hummingbird
has played in the same tree
all day. I see it hang in air.
Then sharp it flicks
                        sideways
to the lower branch, its red throat
sudden and brief as a sense datum
against the immensity of blue.

In Scotland a flock of eider ducks
lived all through the winter
on the same impossible patch of North Sea.
I'd write at the window, feeding pence
to the wall heater to keep half warm,
peer out through the storm to find them
still there, riding
vertical, the whole flock
rolling and freezing on black water.

How could that place be picked out as a place
to be? What made that piece of darkness
somewhere to come back to? Does the hummingbird
poised at the center of its spinning
world think: *here?*

Flatlanders

We are walking down a road in the Green Mountains
near evening. The air is filled with voices
like gulls wheeling. *How could they get here,*
so far from the sea? And then it seems
these must be voices of children
lost and calling. Or a school yard, maybe.
But how could that be, down this small dirt road?
We come around the curve over the rise to find
sheep, hundreds of them, crying toward the barn,
their rough coats stained red-gold
in the twilight. A small border collie weaves
in and out among them. You give me that familiar
sardonic look, as Vermont settles back
into its earthly, intelligible place.

The Visitant

I lie out on the slant of the worn grey dock,
its old square lines worked down by sun and water.
My scarred surgical knees draw the heat of July
like prize melons swelling in a field.
Three summers I have come to this place.
Slipping carefully down into the cold lake,
I begin to float in a new kind of bliss,
damaged but rejoicing at this icy outer edge
of what is. Alive in the slightest sound of my breath,
I am singled out by the generous sun.
For the first time in years, I find myself able
to stand for a spacious moment without pain,
embraced and lifted up in the radiance.
The lake this morning is suspended and still,
as if its spun-silver disk had just arrived
to take me to some other, painless world.
Only here, in this struggling world, are the loons.
And, far out in the silence, one crimson sail.

First Year Teaching, Boston

I thought it said archangels
but woke to a voice saying change
trains. To the tripledeckers
and wash lines of South Boston,
one orange shirt suspended
in the cold clarity like a flag
of occupation. Each morning
I'd ride out to UMass jeeped up
on coffee and too much Heidegger,
come home falling asleep
on the T. Wake to the Irish
motorman calling Park Street, Park
or the smoky red eye slowly closing
over the Charles. That first fall
I'd buy flowers on the walk home,
center them on my one table
in the trapezoid of strange New
England light. Watch the light
slant through and leave them.

Levels of Being

The elevator door slammed shut as usual.
After ten seconds everything went
black. For an instant there was the brain alone
in its own dark box. Then there was the body,
in a larger dark box.
Then the elevator, surrounded by its still
larger box. And the brain thinking loud,
the self condensed to this small startled motion
walled up alone in the Chinese puzzle
revealed by a moment's failure of light.

Inside, Outside

How the lighted inside
of a bus looks from out-
side on a rainy night.
Intimate. Exclusive.
The dirty glass is streaked
with long diagonals
of water. Two people
riding the bus besides
the driver. Silences.
Wipers' hesitant scrape.
The smell of damp wool coats
and the metallic tang
of air inside the bus.
Misting the cold thick glass
with her breath she thinks that
wet streets outside sound so
empty under the wheels
empty under the wheels.

Loving the Clay

— to SELMA BURKE, *sculptor*

In his letters to Theo, Vincent writes how he
looks for blue all the time. Most beautiful
was the coarse linen the peasants wove themselves,
warp black, woof blue. Though no one ever saw
Chardin at work, it was rumored he applied
that thick, buttery pigment with his fingers.

Asked at eighty-eight why she became a sculptor,
Selma Burke described a day when she was five.
Sent down to the riverbed for clay
to make whitewash, she had run back with a life.
What she had seen, clear and fateful in the plain
river mud, was the shape of her own hand.
Asked if she had tried to be a role model
to her people, she said no, she'd never had any
mission in life, she'd just loved the clay.

A Hunger in the Mind Like Texas

I see you bending over
in the garden, short legs sturdy
and planted in the sun.
You could last all day.
In the precision of this memory
I place my hands thumb to thumb
across your narrow shoulders.
Eye to eye we lay under the slow fan,
sweat cooling again on slippery bodies.
Exotic as okra in Massachusetts
you were home soil to me.
I'd hook my hands in your pockets
to pull you close, your mouth
vivid and original as basil
on August tomatoes. I want to eat
with you at the kitchen table.
Read our poems aloud. Look down
into that wide country
face.   Just once.

Roses Red in the Dark

Imagine them leaning apart to unfold,
each long-legged one spreading
slowly in the warm breath
of the bedroom, on the oak chest
floating repeated in the mirror.
Do you see roses red
in the dark? The eye of memory
yields the color you desire. Wide awake
winter mornings, I hear the light
breaking over everything outside this room.
It was just that oldest dream,
of finally reaching essence.

The Perfect Image of Freedom

We are racketing along
in the cotton fields, radio up loud,
in that old Fiat. My brother Charlie
giggles on the seat beside me.
Sweaty little legs stuck straight out,
he bounces up and down as the car plows
over the muddy ruts beside the field.
"We'll never go back," he says.

Or maybe two years ago, you and me
making love and looking out
the crazy window high up,
to find the housepainter leering in
from the ladder next door.
There we were, two women
with no excuses. Holding each other,
we start to laugh; then miraculously
he laughs, too, hanging on
to the ladder, for dear life.

Tableau Vivant

More freesias, you said, so wonderful
to have the flowers appear.
Meanwhile like hard fields waiting for April,
like the crusted New England winter ground
I lie, staring at the lost
flowers of the mind, the newly planted
garden I left behind in California.
Bougainvillea, passion flower, trumpet vine,
and tender shoots of words just breaking through:
why did I leave my own plenitude
for this cold, parsimonious season with you?
Familiar work to make failure out of love.
How do I learn this strangely arduous labor,
growing my own life and staying through the harvest?

Dog at the Goodbye

How they disappear, with their faces
in shadow as the door closes. Only the one
comes back. Hands on me then, down soft
russet flank, and her tears. Longer, longer.
Screen door opens, run to find her
carrying her things out the door.
Now they speak once more, holding keys.
Outside warm ground beside the rose,
heavy wings and wide bars of light.
Bees linger one by one to stroke the lavender.
Lap sweet water from the metal pail,
she's gone again. Nothing more gets said.

Part Three

Beginning to Write

That year I taught Headstart
there was a boy who never spoke.
He'd fit one thin leg
to the taut bow of his chest
and wait. If you fed him, he ate.
While the others were drawing
he sat completely still,
staring at the crayon
lost in his hand. His solitude
filled the narrow church room,
crowded with children
making pictures of their houses.

I would take him on my lap,
lace my fingers through his
and holding the broken crayon
guide our two hands over
the vast open page. One mark,
two—*That's it, Donnie*—
his hand resisting slightly,
cramping our motion.

Donnie came to me today
as I balked on the brink,

not trusting myself
to make my own first mark.
Skin ashy with neglect,
priceless lapful of woe,
he is the child who will always know
it is not safe to speak.

A Sadness Deep as the Atchafalaya

Since this is a memory, it has already happened.
Repetition can't reach back to undo.
The body still chokes down what cannot
not happen; one life was broken into two.
The pain burns through the small secret
places, out to the bones that beat for air.
The legs are pulled wide, taut as a wishbone,
body's seams stretching not to tear.

The lower Mississippi is broad and shallow.
Heavy with all it carries, it flows
in its slow, muddy curve past New Orleans
to the Gulf. It is the river everyone knows,
chosen by fate, used hard and lived on.
The life that would have been is a deeper river.

Teaching Myself to Read

From the first only saying
made things real. I climbed up word
for word the cliff face of all
four-year-old sorrows, reading
the signs in a heavy sky:
PABST. JAX. COKE. The marvel
was that these big neon signs
(unlike the small signs of home
trouble brewing) could be read.
I'd drag my father's heavy
books down to the floor and hold
Last Man Off Wake Island close
to my eyes for hours. Inching
my finger across magic
black rows, I longed to unlock
that secret syntax and just
read myself out of this world.

Implicature

When my mother cursed me
she was wearing white gloves
as all Southern ladies did
on large occasions.

We were in the red clay
cemetery, us two and Tennessee
Williams, searching for the lost
baby's grave in the hot grass.

Mother stalked the graves,
her skinny cracker body
in that hard green dress, air
gone the high white of noon,

me stumbling along behind her.
Mama, let's just go home.
Let's us just go home.
She turned her toppled face

to me: You don't know how
to love, you never will
know how. Her hacksaw rage
whistled clean to the bone.

Speaking to Gingerware

Lugging the heavy stone
cat with one glass eye
for company, all day I speak
to the cat and Gingerware,
my imaginary friend.

Grondidondy gives me seeds
from the cold red melon.
I plant them, cool and slippery,
in the warm Community
Dark Roast coffee grounds
of his worm bed by the porch.

Under the elephant ears,
behind the warm rain
the cat and Gingerware and I
watch and wait, trying to make
something in that family grow.

For days my dreams are of melons
making themselves underground,
and of how surprised the worms will be
to come upon such sweetness
in their dark and bitter home.

Early Platonism

At nine I thought that all words
must fit this world exactly,
reach out to things and hold them
tethered so they couldn't leave
or lose the only sense they made.
Cat's eye, jack knife, taw.
In the cool shady chicken coop
I'd say the words and shape them
to their things: feather, pencil,
coffee can, bone. But how were names
hooked on to things I couldn't hold:
belief, rain, the Battle of Midway
described in the moth-eaten clippings
left there by my grown-up uncle,
who told me one rainy morning words
had no definite meaning at all,
See for yourself, just go look in any
dictionary, he said. I cried.

Lifelines

—for my parents

My grandfather kept his treasures in a big, black trunk.
He would lay them on the worn cotton bedspread
one by one, smelling of Prince Albert and old man.
Faded sepia postcards saved forty years: the Champs-Elysées,
a railway somewhere in France, the spiky scaffolding
of the Eiffel tower half-risen from a muddy field,
and mountains—mountains!—he had never seen one.
Shipped over to build railroads for the Allied Army,
he had seen these marvelous things for himself
and kept the pictures, thinking to pass them on.
Now the small country life he lived has disappeared.
Those marvels are no longer marvelous.
The brakeman's knowledge of curve and grade,
whole towns along the Illinois Central, pine woods
and blacktop roads, the houses he came home to late at night:
all his soul's intimate geography is gone.

What makes that big, slow river I grew up on
more real than anything here? We learned to spell
its charged, mysterious name along with our own,
proud of the river, of how hard it was
to spell. We chanted the letters in unison:
M-AH-double S-AH-double S-AH-double P-AH.
In our best clothes we could be carried to the levee
to see the big ships slide by. Drive over to Mamou,
it made me laugh, like Bunkie and Opelousas.

On the map saved in my mind the river seems to reach
its shining spread-out fingers through the sand,
down to the gulf like the not quite blue
rivers from the heart that run through the hand.

The Word 'Class' Should Not Appear in the Poem

With everything crucial there is danger of mythology, with origins the deepest danger. Don't make a mythology of this: Umah rocking in the porch swing, hands moving quietly in the poetry of snap beans. The rattle of the beans falling into the tin pan. Grondidondy leaning over looking at his heavy high-topped shoes: the reason I don't write you at school is, I can't write so good. And all around us that sweet heavy curtain of Louisiana rain, making a spattering sound on the tin roof, a deeper drumming on the elephant ears. The afternoon rain a familiar room around us.

I had ridden home from school on the train. Sat by a woman named Opal Hart, who kept talking to me as we traveled down through Carolina. When I told her I studied philosophy she wanted to tell me her troubles. I wanted to read. I remember she said she was taking her husband's body back to Indiana. It was the last thing she could ever do for him, that dear man, after two hard years of nursing him all alone. I heard every grammatical mistake, could not stop hearing every trite expression she called up to encompass her sorrow. I kept wincing into my thick book all the way to Waycross, Georgia.

When I got home and was sitting with my grandparents on the porch listening to the rain, Grondidondy tried to tell me again how important my education was. I sat there grieving. He was so proud. All the shame was mine.

Part Four

What Keeps Me Here

—*for* ANNE

Four pine siskins fly
toward me through a bounded field
of light. They flash across
the sharp edge the darkness makes,
arc once, then disappear
into the welter of shadow,
the sweet frayed skins
of eucalyptus on the ground.
I know I would be dead now,
but for this gift. This single
aptitude for celebration.
The other gifts are going.
Hegel's gone. What reaches
for me now: the absurd
dolor of the hound,
the infinite milky ribbon
of the tide, the way
the old pine and the cypress
lean together into the evening
light like two people
going home.

The Problem of Personal Identity

What sorts of characteristics identify a person
as *essentially* the person she is, such that if those
characteristics were changed, she would be a
significantly different person, though she might still
be differentiated and reidentified as the same?
—AMELIE RORTY

Philosophers worry like this.
How many cells have to change
before we refuse to call you
the same woman? How shall we name
what stays the same?

The truth is, pain disintegrates
whatever it embraces.
I keep forgetting to hold
body and soul together.
Like children they go wandering,
they come back different.

For suppose that $S_1, S_2, \ldots$ are person stages; and
suppose that C_1 is the continuant person of whom S_1
is a stage, C_2 is the continuant person of whom S_2 is
a stage, and so on. Then any two of these stages S_i
and S_j are I-related if and only if the corresponding
continuant persons C_i and C_j are identical.
—DAVID LEWIS, *"Survival and Identity"*

For all I know, this is the solution.
I have a different problem.

If pain is the hammer, the body is the anvil.
Where in this is the spirit? The hammer
has come down too many times. I don't live any more
by holding on.

Is this the same woman? Holding my loss
to my ear like a shell, I listen
to the voice of years. The body
is a problem. It must be solved again
each day. What stays the same?

I am back at the beginning with that hunger.
Back to the great happiness of words.
I am stripped to a stubborn heritage
that can outlive pain:
My hands that talk in air
are my grandmother's, knotted and wide
and plain as Mississippi.

Just Before the Dove Begins to Call

Just before the dove begins to call
if you are close you hear
a whir, a small change in air
almost mechanical, like the sound
of a stop opening. This is right
before the short elided call,
that grieving umlaut, not the full
five-tone song. After the call dies,
after that lapse from the brief
cosmos of sound comes a silence
lasting seconds. Then you hear
again the highway in the distance.

Forsan et Haec Olim Meminisse Iuvabit

In Berkeley men have begun to brood
on the streets together by ten in the morning.
The smell of burned coffee fills the neighborhood.
On public radio a man tells how starving
families barely survive 1300 feet above La Paz
chipping at the rock for bricks.
I am waiting for the light at Alcatraz.
A woman starts to cross the street, she walks
leaning way back as if her own knees
were pulling her along. Red socks,
baggy red sweater over a skirt, loafers
and a neat grey bun. Though my throat aches
with sorrow, I find myself smiling in the goofy
unexpected joy of it. I think of the week
in Truro after my last operation. Foggy
all morning, the day had cleared. I walked
to the window over the bay, thinking of my book
about privacy and pain. Stood unseeing
there for a long time.   Oh look,
how the seals' heads glisten in the sun!

The Painful Kingdom of Time and Place

MILLS COLLEGE, 1990

Reading Whitman late into the night *(I know I am solid
    and sound)*
until the gunfire starts again outside the college gates.
    Two long bursts,
then nothing in the dark but silence. Inside these high
    sharpened fences
there is no jeopardy in shadows, in the sigh and whisper
    of expensive trees.
A woman's high thin voice begins to scream and stops
    abruptly. You hear that
broken sound all night. Morning comes like reverie, foggy
    and serene.
Here in faculty village a little boy makes distant popping
    sounds of war
with his mouth as he plays alone. Mirrored silver in the pond,
    one young blue heron
perfects his leggy balance, fanning gravely to keep himself
    upright.

Children Burned in Midnight Fire,
Story at Eleven

Lover, we're going to tear down that flickering city
in which you sleep like a fist curled up and turned away,
back bowed   wholly impervious   braced for trouble
you keep trying   to hide in your body   in the bed
as the hermit   demented in the park   hides
in his language   or the terrorist
slipping like a knife   through the swarming
alleyways.   You in there.   Release your hostages.
Send them all out first,   then you.   Come out real slow.

Declension From Blue

Driving north from Oakland after class,
I'm getting so old, and suddenly
Mt. Tam shows blue in the black notch
of the trees. I have to look. There,
the humped blue backs of the hills
and the light just after, a thin strip
silver behind their surprising indigo.
Then a moment's declension from blue
to purple, a violet haze like a bruise.
Above it deep rose, streaked through
with mauve, orange and clear vermilion.
As I swing east toward Albany and home,
the sky is turning to smudged plum.
Tiny lights go on against the hills.

Afternoon Nap With Pain Meds

My white shirt turned into laundry
flapping in the wind, the crooning sound
beneath the wind was the distant phone
ringing and ringing through the dream
of how it felt to run down the hill,
to kneel in lawns of deep cold clover
with real knees. I could see them
clearly—sturdy, familiar banged-up things
to bandaid, to admire, to rely on.

But here I am awake, thick lids, fat tongue.

Dreaming the Tree of Life

—for CHANA BLOCH

So close I have to lean back to see it.
Nothing will stay still. Each branch I look at
constellates, becomes a finer web of stars.
Its huge crown rises to an astounding whiteness.
Where there should be xylem, phloem,
the trunk is streaming tracers
in the dark. Lights like childhood
flare up and fall down. They make the soft
regretful sounds of Roman candles.
The smallest leaves have turned to flame.

A man stands watching from the shadows.
His glasses gleam as if edged by fire.
He says the tree's life consists in light,
entirely. Says the tree is dying,
beginning to die. He is making a study of it.
The arching branches start to fade
like phosphor, and the stars fall silent.

Grief roots me in the dark place.
Just as I am coming to learn
how the light inside makes the tree live.
Then, a different voice starts speaking quietly
as if inside my head: *Karen, this is the tree of lights.*
Begin at the beginning, exactly in the space
its life left behind in the dark.

"I Will Not Let Thee Go
Except I Bless Thee"

If to lose teaching was a little death
rehearsal, I did it badly. Refusing grief,
using all my thought to hold on tight,
I could not accept that I was not the same
as what I had worked so hard to become.

I had to feel that cherished self break
to understand my beloved philosophers,
Socrates, Epicurus, Montaigne, Weil:
one has to learn how not to be a slave,
how not to cling to what can be let go.

Now like Emily Dickinson, who praised
Jacob as both "pugilist and poet,"
I am trying to live a whole, brave human life
in the spacious seconds after
the blow that counts has already fallen.

In Praise of the Visible World

—for JOEY

The truck driver has blond hair like Stephen's,
soft and baby-fine. From three car lengths behind,
I see it shine out over and over, as the wind lifts his light
    curls.
Merleau-Ponty was right: we see with the whole body,
not just the eyes. The bowl in the painting has a heft
we can estimate by forearm and wrist,
as the surface of the chased and burnished cup
is felt across the room, by means of the hands.
The shiny glaze on the raku-fired pot looks
smooth and cool to the eye as it must be
to the tips of the fingers, as hard to sight as soon
it will feel to the slight, inquiring tap of the knuckle.

His bright hair seen from this distance on the highway
ripples as the wind blows through the cab of his truck,
and I know his hair is thin and light as breath against my
    face.
When that shadow appears at the hollow of your hip, I know
precisely how your warm soft skin will feel
against the grainy whorls at the heel of my hand,
as bending your lips to the head of the sleeping child
you feel what you will find before you find it,
the sweet, familiar scent that rises from his sleep,
a feeling that is knowledge without effort or forethought,
as watching the generous curve of your mouth
years before I kissed you, I knew, before I knew.

The Power to Survive

Woke up in Menlo Park with the highway
sounds that roar and sigh like a sea,
thinking I heard the Berkeley foghorn
near my old house. Just past the edge
of hearing, like coming awake slowly
in the neighborhood of that loved voice.
Its two husky notes always sound the same,
high and then lower, that first flat pitch still
held in the ear when the second is begun.
They hang together in the dense wet air
like the two wistful notes of Shreveport
neighbors whistling every evening
for their children. They always held
that first high note just longer than you thought
they would or could, one extra heartbeat
so that tone seemed to pass straight into
memory's own foggy and capacious harbor,
even while it was still sounding.

That Lighter Journey We Begin at the End

—for my sister, JOAN

My vision of hell is the large moving van
I am condemned eternally to pack and unpack
as payment for my middle-aged foolishness.
Twice I moved my heavy household coast to coast
and right back, unwilling to give anything up.
Possessions battered from being crated,
friends lost, things bent beyond straightening.
All for learning: if you're here, you can't be there.
The teaching job in Massachusetts costs you
the soft hills of Texas. The weather you must have
to ease your bones means you lose
those open, quizzical faces of your students
back in Boston. Only the angels,
lacking bodies, move without suffering loss.
Once encumbered, we never leave lightly.

But maybe all this choosing was a way to evade
the only journey we can't help making.
Once on a bus in Dime Box, Texas,
a woman who had flagged us down
said to the driver as she sat close behind him
and unpinned her hat, One place
is as good as another when the heart
grows cold. What's that? the driver
said, glancing back in the mirror.
One place is as good as another, she said.

THE WAY TO BE IMMORTAL: The quotation at the end is from Sir Thomas Browne, *Religio Medici*, I, 55.

ROSES RED IN THE DARK: This poem started off as a meditation in the dark on remark 515 of Ludwig Wittgenstein's *Philosophical Investigations.*

A SADNESS DEEP AS THE ATCHAFALAYA: The Atchafalaya is a river in south Louisiana, a distributary of the Mississippi. In the natural course of things, the Mississippi would choose the Atchafalaya channel as its shortest course to the sea, but the U.S. Army Corps of Engineers is preventing it.

FORSAN ET HAEC OLIM MEMINISSE IUVABIT: The title is from the famous passage in Book One of Virgil's *Aeneid* in which Aeneas comforts his men after the storm: "Perhaps some day it will be pleasant to remember even these things."

"I WILL NOT LET THEE GO . . ." The idea and the title came from one of Emily Dickinson's last letters. The paragraph reads, "Audacity of Bliss, said Jacob to the Angel 'I will not let thee go except I bless thee'—Pugilist and Poet, Jacob was correct—".